My Teacher's Name Is

Grief

Madeleine Miehls

Illustrated by Adam Perzanowski

For

Emily Cormier

But if you or someone you know deserves a book dedication,

please write the name here:

_____

Do you know what the word GRIEF means? The thesaurus says grief can be "misfortune" or "sorrow."

Some people call it a bleeding heart, a blow, a setback or a tragedy. Anyone who has lost someone they love will tell you it's all of these.

But grief is even more. It's a teacher if we let it be, and a good one. We can actually learn a lot from the sadness that we feel sometimes, not when we're in the middle of grief, but later with time when we feel a little less sad.

Look around you. Everything has a life. It's born, it lives and eventually it disappears. Cut a tomato and eat it. It's there, but then it's gone. The sun rises. The sun sets.

Everything is always changing.

Spring wanes to let Summer start, then Fall comes along, and finally Winter's chill rushes in. Everything changes all the time.

Have you ever watched a clock tick time by? One second, two seconds, three, then five and so on. Poof. A minute has passed. It will never come back.

Once again, something starts, is here for a time and then it is gone.

These changes are like mini-deaths in some ways...but death is a big change.

Maybe a grandparent or mom or dad dies. Or perhaps it's a spouse, a sibling, a child or even a pet that we lose.

It hurts. And the pain is felt deep within us.

But we can learn a lot from the grief we experience.

The ache we feel in our gut that makes us want to claw at the wall or scream or cry on someone's shoulder...it's a teacher.

It doesn't look like the ones we have at school. No skirt or slacks – not standing at the chalkboard, but it's there with a lesson.

We can't escape sorrow. We might point to friends and say, "They have the perfect family." Perhaps to you it looks intact, complete, with a mother, father, kids and even a goldfish. And there's probably a kid in school you can name who gets all As and a neighbor with the best looking flowerbeds and someone you recall from work who almost effortlessly receives promotions and awards.

Well, perfection is really an illusion. It doesn't last. At some point, things that are will no longer be. Somebody dies. There are no exceptions. Money, fame, charm – even they cannot prevent it.

What can grief do for us? What does it offer besides a bad time and a sick stomach?

Well, it helps us remember.

When we're sad, we think about all the memories we have about a person or pet we loved and lost.

And we can save those memories in our mind, in scrapbooks through pictures and in words too if we write them down.

Doing so gives us comfort and helps us bond in a special way with the person we lost by keeping memories of them alive in our hearts.

And years later, whether we are feeling happy or sad, we can return to those images whenever we want.

But first we must walk on a road and it is not an easy journey. There are lots of bumps along the way.

Are you willing to walk?

Stick with it and don't give up. You will learn a lot while "on the road."

Who have you lost that you love?

Think about that for a moment.

Really think.

How did you feel when you found out the person or pet was gone – had died?

Shock is how most people describe it.

And it's scary isn't it?

When I was a kid, my great grandma died. She was a cool lady and lived to be 95 years-old. She was born in 1876, a long time ago.

She told stories about Indians on the "plains" where she lived. They came up to her house and asked for corn-on-the-cob when she was a child.

I can still remember special times we shared at her house on the St. Clair River near Port Huron, Michigan.

Sometimes we'd sit on the lawn near the river and try to match the passing freighter smoke stack symbols with the companies they represented. Then afterward I'd help her roll sheet bandages for the soldiers in the Vietnam War.

On other occasions, she read me the comics from the newspaper. We often sat at the kitchen table together. My job: turn the pages. Grandma's job: read the words, point out the funniest pictures and laugh – a loud chuckle that left me giggling. It was a happy time.

I was sitting in the front foyer of our home when my mom came in to tell me about my grandma's death. And I remember laughing as she retold old stories and put an arm around me. She laughed too. Then in a flash I got quiet and felt a little guilty.

Someone had died. Should I feel joy?

My smiles faded and I grew frightened.

Why? Because I suddenly realized that if grandma died, I could die too. And that was a scary thought. And I wanted to know if I'd live to see seven, or ten, or to get my first car or move into my sister's bigger bedroom, which had two windows and a huge closet.

And then I had nothing but crazy thoughts, until my mom called me back into the kitchen to do a job: set the table for dinner.

Whenever somebody dies it's scary. And it's permanent. Maybe that's what makes it so scary. And we never expect it. Even if someone is really sick, don't you just hold out for a little hope – that maybe, they'll pull through? I always thought that way as a kid. But one day that started to change.

My mom got sick when I was in seventh grade. She had breast cancer and it was serious. There was lots of whispering in the house, and I got shuffled to a grandparent's home where I heard more whispering on the telephone. And every time I asked, "What's going on?" everybody said, "Nothing." If there's one thing a kid hates – it's being told nothing, when there is obviously something going on.

My mom died during my senior year of high school. And even though I knew it would happen – because she told me so, I was frightened.

I trembled.

I felt afraid and alone and wondered, "Will I be next?" I was into order, and according to my rules, once mom died, I could be next…or my sister or brother I guess. Dad couldn't. He had to work to pay the bills. But in my view I was dispensable and the youngest—a very likely target.

And when she died I became unmoored, no longer tied to the person I loved so much. My boat was floating without a captain and I felt like a marionette with cut strings. I didn't want to be "free." I wasn't old enough to steer. I wanted a mom and dad to chart my course.

But one of my captains was gone – forever.

It's almost too hard to imagine a parent or spouse or other person who you are close to, with you, and then suddenly "poof" as if a magician has waved a wand and moved a curtain, they are gone, forever.

I panicked.

I screamed.

I cried.

I was sad.

I had no one to talk to that I trusted.

I felt very alone.

I wanted my mom back.

I screamed at God.

I held her nightgown in my hands and I wept.

And I wept some more.

And still more tears came.

Then I started to question my own life.

When would I die?

What was God's plan for me?

Why didn't God's blueprint include the person I loved – the person I lost?

So many questions and no immediate answers.

When we see someone we love die or hear about it, it's natural to wonder what will happen to us going forward into the future without this person.

Sometimes it feels like part of you goes with the person who dies. In fact, it can feel like all of "you" is gone, not just a part — but as though two people died.

I felt that way when I lost my mom to cancer.

Yes, I was alive, not dead...but just the same, I figured...geez somebody save me...don't let me die. I wanted to save both of us.

But to "go on" I had to let someone go.

And so I did.

When someone dies we often greet the news with "It just can't be." And if you believe in God like I do, you might wonder how a kind and loving God could allow something so cruel to occur.

That's how I felt when my mom passed away.

I screamed, "NO, it can't be happening," because I didn't want to accept what really was.

It's never easy to give up someone we love, no matter how strong or brave we are.

And when we know the person will be gone forever, that we'll never see the person in this life again, it can feel impossible.

And yet, when somebody dies we're asked to do just that.

After a time, and I can't say how long that time is – you cannot measure it on a clock in units of minutes or hours, anyhow, you will start to feel just a little different. I won't say better. I say different because what happens is really up to you. Grief will start to "work" on you. And you will start to "work" on grief. It's like homework, in the sense that you didn't ask for the assignment, you probably don't want to do it, but know you must – because that's how you learn.

Grief teaches you, just a little at a time. You don't feel warm sunlight or spot rainbows. At first all you see are clouds and rain — it's dark and damp and eerie.

What do you do? You listen. You watch, and you move.

That last part is really important.

You move.

To get through the sadness that grief ushers in, you can't sit in a chair in your bedroom and expect to feel like yourself in a day or two or even a month. You have to get up and leave the room. It's okay to take little steps, tiny little steps, but you need to move. Nobody can move you. This is your assignment, not a friend's.

First steps might involve finding people who share similar interests and circumstances, joining a book club you've heard about but never investigated, sampling great pizza at a new downtown restaurant, taking a vacation, or meeting up with a friend from the past, one you've forgotten about – until now. Like they say in chess: it's your move.

What happens as you move along with Grief the teacher at your side? You start to see what you had and understand what it means to you, and at the same time you start looking ahead…just to get a little peek at what excitement might be around the next bend. All the while, you keep a watchful eye on happenings around you, with a heightened sense of import.

Yes, you hurt.

And yet you start to heal.

What now?

You watch.

You move.

You cry a lot.

You try new things.

You remember.

You cry.

You try more new things.

You cry a little less.

What now?

It's still your move.

Months after my grandma's death, I saw a funeral procession with cars inch through Rochester, Michigan one day while running errands with my mom. And immediately, I felt sad for the people in the cars lined up behind the hearse.

Why? They had lost someone, just like me. And I felt connected with those people as they drove by, even though I'd never met them and never would.

I felt their pain. We were the same in that way. We had the same pain: the pain of loss. So grief taught me compassion for others. And by caring for them in some little way, I felt it for me too.

But the only reason I felt better was because I chose to. And you have a choice too. You can let grief run you and your life and if you do, it will hold you back, or it can be your teacher, your guide. Smart people, and I think you are smart, will let it teach—will choose to let it teach.

When someone dies, we'd all like a little magic fairy dust or a machine to take us back in time. But it doesn't work that way.

We can't control all life's circumstances, but we can control our reactions to them.

You can hole up in a bedroom or avoid leaving your yard. Maybe someone died in a car crash and now you are afraid to sit in a vehicle. That's understandable.

But don't give in. Don't give up.

Just keep plugging way, one step at a time, one breath, one thought, one second. You can do it. You'll be happy again, IF YOU CHOOSE IT.

But the good and happy feelings you will have won't be like before. You'll be smarter, and your happiness will be really special. Why? Because you'll truly understand that nothing lasts forever.

Maybe you'll spend more time thinking about today
instead of worrying about tomorrow.

Maybe you'll laugh more, smile more and be with people more.
Maybe you'll ….

What is grief's lesson? What do we get?

Yes, it hurts to lose something we love. But the facts are that it will happen to us at some point in our lives.

So what do we get in return for all the pain we suffer? Is there a winner? What do they win?

We grow — that's the prize. I know you probably thought there would be something great, like a lifetime supply of candy or an electronic wonder toy.

But the truth is: you get a lesson – a life lesson that ultimately teaches you to ENJOY EVERY SINGLE DAY because you don't know what tomorrow will bring.

Okay, seriously, what is the *real* lesson?

That eventually you'll stand on your own feet and serve others with care and compassion. You will no longer need to define yourself through titles like "mother", "father", "sibling" or "daughter" because on your journey you will discover new definitions of "you" and more will unfold in the future.

Best of all, you will take what you know no matter how old you are – NOBODY wants to lose someone they love – and you'll give it away. One day your grief experience will be a gift, one you give to someone else who hurts.

And when you can do that, with love, without pause, you will be healed.

Don't wrap a cage around your heart forever. Live and love and laugh again. Work at it – walk step by step with grief as your guide, and you will.

It's hard to see the beauty of a storm when you are in the middle of it. Have you ever seen pictures of tornados on television or in a book? Some people are awestruck by their magnitude and dare I say it, beauty. Yes, there is often wreckage in the tornado's path, but many people are drawn to pictures of nature, doing its thing.

Now think for a moment. If your house got wrecked by a tornado would you call it beautiful? No, of course not.

But what if you were a photographer standing in a corn field watching a storm from afar with the sun at your back?

Would it look better to you then?

Grief is a lot like that. It's impossible to see beauty and awe when you are in the middle of it, but with distance — with time, you get perspective, a special viewing angle that shows you not just how far you've come, but what you've learned along the way.

As we age we gain experience. If you are young, you don't have the mileage of an adult. And if you are older and haven't experienced grief before, you might feel like a child inside. Know that loss is a necessity of living. We all get hit with it. Nobody who truly lives and loves another can avoid it.

We will love some living breathing thing, give it our heart and one day, it will pass away and be gone. Don't stop loving even when there is loss. As something ends you will find new beginnings: a life worth living and more people worth loving.

It doesn't get better than that...well maybe it does. You'll smile.

✱✱✱✱✱✱✱✱

A Note to the Reader From the Author Madeleine Miehls

I want to share some of my thoughts with you. Odds are that you are reading this book because you have lost someone you love. I don't know you. And you don't know me. But, you are holding this book and reading it and I wrote it. So together we share a special bond: yes, we share the book *and* the pain of loss. Now, in some small way we are connected to each other. Thank you for letting me share what I learned from grief. I hope you one day can share your knowledge too.

Please know that grief is not an easy process. It's hard work. But good comes from it if we let it - if we work with it. I know. I'm a survivor. It's true I lost my mom when I was 16 – to cancer, and I lost a husband later to the same disease. Our daughter was four years-old at the time. It's also true that I miscarried four times between our daughter's birth and my husband's diagnosis. After hearing that you might say, "Good God, how did she do it? How did she get through it?" Well you already answered it when you said, "Good God." God got me through it, little by little. But I had work to do too. It wasn't all God and it wasn't all me. One step at a time I trudged along, trusting in God, trusting that there was a future, knowing there would be setbacks along the way. Well, I am here and I am happy.

I can honestly tell you that I am a better person for having loved people in my life even if I had to lose them, than I ever could have been without them. Each influenced me in some way. And grief made an imprint on me too. I don't talk about my husband in the text, but I will say a few words here. Did I love him? Absolutely. Do I miss him? Yep. But there are many adventures I would not have taken if my husband was still alive. I did so many things – afterward, without him. I did them because of him. Loss frightened me and simultaneously made me incredibly brave. Read the list. Think. I want to give you hope in tomorrow.

The Adventure

I took Irish dancing lessons with my daughter. We danced in front of 2,000 people and made new friends. We are not even Irish, but it sure was fun! I started a marketing and technical writing consulting business, www.WriteSideOfBusiness.com and now I work with people all over the United States, even globally! I drove my daughter across the country to more states than most people can name, in just 35 days – 10,000 miles in all. I appeared on television for work I do. I made a lot of new friends – and yes, I lost some old friends. That can happen when you become widowed. I offered grief support for a few years in and around the Detroit area for a group called Widowed Friends (www.WidowedFriends.org), a great organization, and spoke at their retreat. I joined the Small Business Association of Michigan and other groups to network with people both socially and professionally. I wrote this book and have two more in the works.

Get the idea? Life is worth living. You will hurt. You will cry and for a time people will bend an ear. Then one day they won't. We are a forward looking society. It's okay to look back, but not to take up residence there. Eventually you have to move on, and live. Nobody will do it for you. But faith in God sure helps! Without my faith I would not be where I am today. Remember, it's all about choice, a choice you make. What do you want? Happiness...or the other option. That second one didn't work for me.

AuthorHouse™
1663 Liberty Drive
Bloomington, IN 47403
www.authorhouse.com
Phone: 1-800-839-8640

©2010 Madeleine Miehls. All rights reserved.

No part of this book may be reproduced, stored in a retrieval system, or
transmitted by any means without the written permission of the author.

First published by AuthorHouse 12/28/2010

ISBN: 978-1-4567-1453-6 (sc)

Printed in the United States of America

Any people depicted in stock imagery provided by Thinkstock are models,
and such images are being used for illustrative purposes only.
Certain stock imagery © Thinkstock.

This book is printed on acid-free paper.

Because of the dynamic nature of the Internet, any Web addresses or links contained in this book may have changed
since publication and may no longer be valid. The views expressed in this work are solely those of the author and do not
necessarily reflect the views of the publisher, and the publisher hereby disclaims any responsibility for them.